Introducing Focus

The Ultimate Guide to Achieving Unbreakable Focus, Increasing Your Productivity, and Sharpening Your Mind

By David Spencer

Copyright @2018 David Spencer

All rights reserved. No part of this book may be reproduced in any form or by any means without permission in writing from the publisher, .

If you like my book, please leave a positive review on Amazon. I would appreciate it a lot. Thanks! This is the link:

<u>**Leave your review here. Thank you!**</u>

Contents

Chapter 1 - Focus Defined

Focus is vital to achievement. It might really fall in an indistinguishable class from aspiration, inspiration, authority and other main impetuses behind getting to be effective, however does not really get the consideration that it merits. Frequently minimized, the part of focus can't be disrupted in a person's capacity to be beneficial.

What this essentially implies is that you should be engaged keeping in mind the end goal to accomplish something or end up effective in your tasks. In any case, before we go into that, here is a glance at what concentrate truly implies.

By definition, focus is an ability that enables individuals to begin an assignment without dawdling and after that keep up their consideration and exertion until the point that the activity is finished. It is a capacity to not just focus on things that they are occupied with yet in addition stay away from diversions that will block the work they are attempting to do.

Truth be told, focus is so essential to completing anything that you can't generally think without focus. When you catch wind of things like discernment, memory, getting the hang of, thinking, basic leadership and critical thinking, you realize that none of these should be possible effectively unless you focus.

Despite what might be expected, a meandering personality will make you less viable in your work and your efficiency will endure. A similar will likewise trade off the nature of work giving you not as much as ideal outcomes. Not to overlook that you will likewise be sitting idle each example your mind floats off.

Why Do We Suffer A Lack of Interest?

Now and again, an absence of focus might involve intrigue. Take your regular plan for the day for example. Not everything on the rundown may enthusiasm to take a shot at, however needs to complete in any case for you to push forward. In these cases you may get yourself stuck, caught accomplishing something that you couldn't think less about. Your exclusive commitment might be the inclination that you have to take care of business to proceed onward to different things. Not such an extraordinary help, but rather such is life; in reality things need to complete to clear a path for different things.

It is just regular that your mind begins to float off in these circumstances. You may wind up discovering excuses for not doing that specific thing, say by defending that you don't generally need to carry out the activity right at that point, or that it's not by any stretch of the imagination that critical or notwithstanding something like you have preferable activities over the activity close by. Be that as it may, any way you dress them up, they are on the whole just reasons for delaying.

Which conveys us to another part of focus; delaying. Dawdling is maybe the greatest obstacle in the method for accomplishing great core interest. When you utilize lingering to escape things you are truly saying that you would prefer not to complete a specific job, or that you are secretly trusting that it will simply leave without anyone else, or that you will in the long run feel roused to do it.

With such a great amount of going on, it is no big surprise that concentration gets sidelined and never surfaces to the cutting edge.

And keeping in mind that significantly more can be said on hesitation, we will cross that extension when we come to it (in a later part). For the present, it is adequate to state that lingering, truth be told, is the granddaddy of all reasons and will never give you a chance to focus legitimately around any given assignment.

How Might You Counter A Lack of Focus?

Proceeding onward, while you might be very much aware of what is preventing you from focusing (think tarrying), you may not know how to handle this issue. So, here's some assistance:

- Address WHAT should be finished

To influence focus to work for you, you need an obvious objective; call it a grounded reason towards which every one of your endeavors are coordinated. When you have this reference point in locate, you can apply all your range of abilities and basic leadership to take care of business right. Yet, with this pivotal factor missing, you should go on a crazy ride.

It is these obvious objectives that characterize the main priority.

Obvious objectives likewise prevent you from crashing and keep you from going spots where you never expected to go. Select a common day in your life and think about all the fifty or so things you have to do. With your mind separated and scattered endeavoring to manage every one of the fifty in the meantime, you are likely not going to complete much. On the other side, you may really disregard to do a portion of the more essential ones as you continue contemplating everything else.

This is where focus can come spare your day. Utilizing focus, work by the procedure of disposal and organize your objectives. When you figure out how to organize your objectives, you wind up investing your energy in a more significant manner; the essential stuff completes first and the not really critical later on.

Sifting through such time-eaters additionally enable you to recover control over confusion and you never again feel that you are dawdling.

•   Address WHY something needs to be done

At the point when obvious objectives are matched with a feeling of purpose, the problem begins to determine itself pretty effortlessly. This sense of purpose also verifies why something needs to be done.
People are naturally more motivated when they have a reason to do something. With that reason in mind, you

will feel more inclined to perform better so you can get the results you seek. A sense of purpose will also fine tune your focus as you want to get the best results out of your efforts.

- Also address WHEN something needs to be done

This one ties in with prioritizing your goals so that important things get done first. Knowing when to do what can make everyday living so much easier to cope with.

Plus, giving yourself a timeframe to work within helps you stay on task i.e. stay focused so you can then have more time to do the other things you need to do.

Successful time management lets you take control of your life rather than follow others. Plus, you end up accomplishing more, performing better and becoming more successful at what you do. Added perks include a sense of satisfaction and peace of mind.

But whether it is prioritizing goals, finding a sense of purpose or practicing time management skills, none of it can be achieved without good focus.

Having set up that being able to focus is a critical component for accomplishment in life, let us now investigate the distinctive sorts of focus you have to develop to make that progress.

Inner focus

This is the most common of all types. Inner focus is an individual's ability to block our distractions, focus on the present moment and task and stay calm under the pressure. This type of focus develops a person's intuition, gut feeling and good decision making.
The benefit of establishing inner focus allows to stay focused in your goals and manage your own schedule.

Focusing on others

Not everyone masters this type of focus as it goes beyond what you are doing and demands that you attend to what others are doing and saying instead. This type of focus is especially important in workplace situations or teamwork scenarios where your output is affected by others' input. However, this type of focus is not only restricted to professional settings, but is equally applicable to personal and social contexts as well.

Outer focus

Outer focus goes beyond paying attention to other people and demands paying attention to your surroundings instead. Outer focus is based on peripheral learning and allows a person to think strategically. It also allows for making adjustments to outer surroundings as circumstances around you change.

Being overpowered brings about burnout. This creates a condition where the individual feels rationally, sincerely and physically depleted. The inclination happens when you feel overpowered and aren't ready to stay aware of requests. Accordingly tumult additionally factors into the condition and the missing component by and by is focus.

The sentiment being diligently overpowered can without much of a stretch reason you to lose enthusiasm and additionally inspiration and expedite an express that abandons you feeling frail, defenseless and amazingly exhausted. By and by, you might attempt to do excessively significantly more than it is practical to deal with.

When discussing burnout, recall that it isn't minor weariness that you encounter. It doesn't only influence your execution yet every part of life. For example, work may end up agonizing, yet you will likewise lose enthusiasm for nearly everything else that you do. Fun quits being fun while each irrelevant thing begins to trouble you.

In a condition of burnout, this inclination does not leave but rather sticks around all the time. Truth be told, remaining in this hopeless condition will probably influence you to trust that there is no option or escaping this chaos.

So how would you get yourself out of this groove? You turn your regard for focus.

Keep in mind what being engaged shown you in the past section? The WHAT, WHY and WHEN recipe will come in extremely convenient when you feel overpowered. Deal with issues by concentrating on what's vital, make sense of why it is so and when to manage it. When you have the responses to these straightforward inquiries you can at any rate begin to unravel the web of feeling overpowered.

Nonetheless, the issue with feeling overpowered is that it isn't generally conceivable to recognize the burnout yourself. Specialists suggest that when feeling troubled, search out assistance from companions, family and others that you trust. They can give you an outside feeling as well as have the capacity to enable you out by referring to cases of why they to trust you might be worn out.

Focus to Fix the Impacts of the Burnout

When you have recognized the trigger for your burdens, be set up to roll out some genuine improvements. This exertion will take a great deal of spotlight on your part as you won't just need to roll out genuine improvements yet in addition stay with them for some time. The splendid side to this whole scene is that once you begin making the move, you ought to likewise begin to feel more inspired once more. A decent place to begin is by concentrating and taking a shot at a portion of the accompanying:

• Cut off the wellspring of the burnout-Where conceivable, disregard the trigger that is making you feel overpowered. Employment related burnouts frequently occur from an excessive number of hours working and too minimal individual time.

• Try to be sound Being overpowered can without much of a stretch incur significant injury on well-being, so participate in some type of physical action to offer yourself a reprieve. While taking a break may sound outlandish to focusing, the thought is to move the concentration from the reason for the burnout and divert focus around dealing with yourself.

• Eat well-Focus on dealing with yourself by eating somewhat better than anyone might have expected. Odds are that being in a worn out state, you likewise ignored your eating routine. All things considered, the main thing the vast majority go after when overpowered is a wealth of garbage and accommodation foods. Throw these out and refocus on what will improve you feel both on the all around.

- Sleep better-Last, however not minimum a burnout will deliver long haul weariness with it. The straightforward way of dealing with stress for this issue is to focus around getting both great quality and amount of rest.

When you need to escape this sad state, recall that concentration is the one thing holding everything together. It is this capacity to focus on your prosperity that will enable you to evacuate all the pessimism out of your life.

The Effect of Being Overwhelmed

While you are in an interior condition of being unfocused, things can turn out badly in the outside world. Individual turbulence aside, the world continues moving at its pace, proceeding to besiege you with the everyday routine, moving dangerously fast. With decisions and data heaping up constantly, it turns out to be extremely difficult to remain focused. And keeping in mind that you will most likely be unable to recognize so yourself, there are certain warnings that can recognize the most widely recognized propensities for unfocused individuals:

- They don't design

It is extremely hard to remain focused without an arrangement to execute. Unfocused people tend to work by impulse, as opposed to by system. They appear to get into things that they "think" may be vital without extremely knowing why. Despite what might be expected, individuals who focus around their objectives have a technique to execute and move dynamically through their motivation as opposed to haphazardly.

- They forget about time

In the event that you end up running shy of time on a large portion of your assignments, you are most likely not concentrating on great time administration. You might get too profound into things, where it isn't required and wind up investing excessively energy in one particular errand which, with focus and arranging could have been designated to various tasks.

Being unfocused likewise makes the individual battle with monitoring time.

- They run late

Nearly tying in with poor time administration is the helplessness of continually running late. Unfocused individuals have a tendency to blunder time as well as display unlikely thoughts regarding time.

For example, a typical propensity is to have a vague thought regarding to what extent it takes to get to places. It progresses toward becoming standard with such individuals to miscount separations or disregard outside components that may influence travel times.

Another normal situation of being unfocused is the point at which somebody goes up against another venture without completing a past one. The outcome is only mayhem where relatively few of the activities complete and the individual is left hastening to complete while running behind on different errands.

- They get effectively diverted

Individuals without focus are the most effortless focuses of diversions. In other words that diversions are all around; some of them self-evident, others not so much, but rather they do impede completing things.

On the off chance that you are not focused, at that point each time you change or move starting with one action then onto the next, there is a period slack in the middle. For unfocused people, this void can without much of a stretch be filled by tricky diversions like getting on their PDA, playing treat smash, and even a basic discussion is sufficient to benefit them far from their relegated task. Does that sound like something that transpires a great deal? Provided that this is true, you have to take a shot at your core interest.

- They are untidy, disorderly and conceivably even flaky

Being out of spotlight leaves its blemish on the authoritative abilities of any individual. Such individuals have a tendency to be encompassed by mess, unfit to ever discover what they are searching for and endure gravely with regards to profitability.

They are likewise unfit to complete on guarantees, tend to avoid arrangements and are very inclined to crossing out finally.

Unfocused individuals experience serious difficulties conferring and show up as flaky when they constantly neglect to finish. This damages their endeavors as well as can be tragic for their notoriety.

•   They stress over everything

On the off chance that you find that you stress excessively or get upset over each little thing, you have to divert your spotlight and channel it on things that are really vital. Figure out how to recognize the generous stuff from the inadequate and afterward focus around that by itself.

Since you realize that diversion is the principle reason we lose focus, let us speak somewhat about the different structures diversions can take. As a rule, these diversions may not appear as evident as one envisions but rather may influence you to feel scattered or fluffy. The outcome is that you may wind up reprimanding yourself for not having more control.

Now it is essential to recall that as we get more established, both concentration and focus can change, similarly as so would memory be able to and other subjective capacities. In any case, this does not need to be unavoidable. In actuality, certain investigations with more seasoned people uncover that the limit with respect to vital learning or basic leadership may even enhance with age.

There are sure propensities and circumstances that can factor into hindering core interest. Most are ordinary propensities that that be changed with some exertion and may turn into the beginning stage for you to push forward with increasing better concentration and fixation.

Terrible Diet and Nutrition

Nourishment directly affects perception which is the reason a poor choice at lunch can crash a whole evening. Why this happens is on the grounds that all that we eat is changed over by the body into glucose giving vitality. In any case, only one out of every odd kind of food is prepared by the body at a similar rate.

So a less than stellar eating routine that prompts craving and lack of hydration can turn into a noteworthy diversion. Yearning can have a bunch of negative impacts on well-being and conduct including the capacity to focus. It is regularly fixing in to low glucose that straightforwardly prompts exhaustion and low vitality levels.

Being thirsty, then again can prompt various indications that can decrease focus including cerebral pains, weariness and low temperament. Studies build up that even 1% lower than ideal hydration can realize an absence of core interest.

So what are a portion of the traps you have to maintain a strategic distance from to let craving and drying out from setting in? Here's a look:

•   Weight misfortune slims down

Weight reduction eating methodologies are famously awful for focus and focus. Among these low fat eating methodologies can be considered responsible as the mind needs fundamental unsaturated fats for appropriate working and these fats deny the assortment of such supplements. In the meantime, removing on imperative supplements like proteins is awful too. This is on the grounds that the amino acids in protein are basic for ideal mind execution in making cerebrum chemicals that enhance focus.

•   Processed nourishments

Poor nourishment, regularly as unfilled calories does not give you the vitality that you require. With deficient vitality, the mind experiences serious difficulties working or concentrating on anything appropriately. Accordingly you may find that you encounter mellow crabbiness when you eat prepared foods.

An illustration; eating prepared nourishments, for example, cured meats can make the mind foggy. When you expend salt and protein rich foods like these there is an inclination to wind up got dried out, and drying out can reduce psychological capacity.

• Junk foods

Garbage foods are an entire distinctive story without anyone else's input. Garbage foods arrive in a high-fat, high-sugar and unhealthy bundle that gets processed decently fast. And keeping in mind that you may get moment delight from eating these nourishments, they truly don't do much to fulfill hunger.

Rather, since garbage foods are without supplements, the body gets compelled to connect with sugar as a wellspring of vitality. This type of vitality is rapidly spent given the refined idea of sugar, abandoning you with a sugar rush additionally experienced as an impermanent vibe of vitality.

Be that as it may, after the digestion has spent all the accessible vitality, the surge is trailed by a sugar crash joined by a sentiment weariness, torpidity, focus misfortune and a meandering mind.

Hormones at Play

Keeping up hormonal harmony is critical to ideal cerebrum working. It might amaze you to realize that an insufficiency of particular hormones can achieve critical changes in mental concentration and handling.

With hormones crooked you may wind up experiencing issues recalling individuals' names, snapping unexpectedly, experiencing emotional episodes or even begin to feel discouraged. All these and different components have an impact in influencing the way your cerebrum capacities.

For ladies, the one thing to keep an eye out for is estrogen levels. This female hormone can manage everything from sugar desires and episodes of exhaustion to state of mind swings. Any lopsidedness is then observed as affecting mental nimbleness where low estrogen levels can hinder mental capacities like memory, thinking and even mind-set from running easily.

Therefore ladies may regularly watch that changes in estrogen levels amid perimenopause and menopause may influence their memory and consideration regarding wax and wind down.

Another thought that falls under hormonal irregular characteristics and one that can affect the capacity to focus is hypothyroidism. Low thyroid issues have been straightforwardly connected with causing mental mist, focus issues, melancholy and even here and now memory misfortune.

It is vital that an ideal adjust of estrogen, progesterone and testosterone is kept up since every one of the three hormones act specifically on nerve cells in the mind. By and large, these hormones can help encourage neurotransmission, shield cells from neurotoxins and enhance blood stream in the cerebrum. Any irregularity and the outcome could be a noteworthy drop in perception, mental concentration and the capacity to maintain focus.

Absence of Rest

This basic issue does not get the genuine consideration it merits. Indeed, even with a solitary night of deficient rest, the mind endures significantly and focus progresses toward becoming traded off. When you don't rest soundly, your manners of thinking moderate down and you turn out to be less caution. This influences your capacity to focus and can make the mind sufficiently confounded to keep you from performing errands that require complex idea.

Likewise, feeling drowsy can cut into your working memory which is a vital part of focusing. The sensation makes you less careful and decreases the speed and precision of mental tasks.

While memory and subjective working bit by bit lessen with age, individuals with steady or more elevated amounts of pressure are particularly defenseless. The negative impacts of weight on memory can make the cerebrum solidify and totally forget about core interest. This can occur in any situation from understudies considering for an exam to presenting a companion and overlooking their name mid-route through presentations.

Focus folds under to worry in these circumstances as speculation gets so engrossed with pressure actuating jolts that different considerations neglect to develop. Thusly it hampers working memory which is related with here and now memory.

Standard exercise discharges mind chemicals which are key for memory and an absence of the same can affect focus and fixation. Exercise animates zones of the cerebrum which are engaged with memory capacities. Physical movement discharges a substance called BDNF or mind inferred neuro trophic factor which rewires memory circuits so they work better.

All things considered 30 minutes of activity can help make more BNDF. Be that as it may, doing as such once seven days won't help. Exercise should be made a general piece of day by day routine to receive intellectual rewards.

Surroundings

The earth where you are taking a seat can rapidly turn into a diverting variable when you are attempting to focus. There could be various redirections, for example, noisy clamors, splendid lighting, visual disturbances and even temperature irregularities.

Despite the fact that they may appear to be inconsequential, these ecological factors can assume a vital part in manifesting the deciding moment focus.

Quality of Information

Another normal diversion is the nature of data you have to process. On the off chance that the data is applicable to the job needing to be done, at that point it will probably maintain your concentration drew in yet you can without much of a stretch end up occupied in the event that you don't have the correct data to work with. Issues like a fragmented email, a skipped step or a deceptive telephone message can foul up your concentration as you endeavor to understand the circumstance.

So far it is sheltered to state that being engaged can help yield extraordinary advantages for the psyche and body as well as the general life nature of a man. Here is the means by which being engaged can enable you to make more noteworthy progress and control of your life:

Enables Take to Control

When you are engaged, you can take control of the things that you are doing. However, in the event that you are not engaged, that assignment or thing will wind up controlling you. When you end up concentrated on something and you have diverted all your vitality into that specific errand, you can deal with the task better.

Control will likewise come simple when you apply all the three kinds of concentrate at the same time into every one of your errands. Internal spotlight will keep you on track and far from diversions while focusing on others makes you more mindful. In any case, it is maybe external concentration that will be most helpful in picking up control since it gives you the adaptability to give you an emergency course of action if necessary.

Yields Positive Vitality

Being engaged helps collect positive vitality in the body. It additionally enables you to get yourself out of a negative winding and place things into point of view.

When you take a gander at various parts of every day life, the intuitive response is to focus on the deficiencies and spotlight on what's off-base.

What's more, since consideration opens up everything, concentrating on the negative perspectives will exacerbate everything. Rather, it is best to withdraw from the issue and reinvest focus around how to make the best out of an awful circumstance.

Ordinary deterrents are an unavoidable event, however when you focus around the positive it can enable you to traverse troublesome circumstances all the more consistently.

Maybe situations like this will request that you draw out your inward concentration completely since such circumstances influences the individual actually. The same can likewise make mayhem throughout everyday life, so concentrating on the positive can help diminish or dispose of this turmoil totally.

Improves Critical Thinking Abilities

A standout amongst the most imperative advantages of remaining focused is that it refines your critical thinking aptitudes. In the event that you are not engaged, you will never endure an issue.

The way an individual methodologies an issue can fluctuate enormously. For example, one individual may concentrate more on the on the reason of the issue than the arrangement, and the other the other way around. The previous of these will have issue focused reasoning while the last will take part in arrangement focused reasoning.

Of the two, issue focused reasoning won't help explain anything besides arrangement focused reasoning can yield the contrary outcome.

Instills Basic Leadership Skills

The capacity to settle on choices is vital for survival and can't be executed without focus. Fruitful basic leadership depends on the

standards of coherent and basic reasoning which should be focus based. Regardless of whether you are a manager or a worker, whether you are a parent or an understudy, you have to settle on a few choices either on everyday schedule or on incidental premise. None of the choices can be made until and unless you are totally focused around the issue.

Furthermore, the issue does not resolve by essentially settling on any choice, but rather it must be the correct one. In addition settling on the correct choice likewise includes executing it effectively. The procedure incorporates distinguishing basic choices and sifting through immaterial ones.

Settling on the correct choice likewise implies you have to focus around getting the correct data to settle on a decent choice.

Removes Distractions

Achievement isn't something that can be accomplished without assurance and self control. To have both these characteristics, you have to focus around disposing of diversions.

While it might appear that individuals who are profoundly sorted out and effective are much the same as everyone, this isn't the situation. Rather, they have a few propensities that are related with the disposal of diversions from their life.

Diversions can remove you from your objectives and points. Indeed, even on everyday schedule, even the most well-known diversion can make the consummation of the task a difficulty. In this manner, you have to remain focused on the grounds that it is just through remaining focused that you can prevail with regards to disposing of diversions.

When you can do that, there is nothing preventing you from accomplishing your objectives or completing your tasks. By the day's end, it generally boils down to how focused you are around your objective. In the event that you ask any well known and effective individual, you would see that concentration was a major piece of their story. This is on the grounds that what you continually focus around will in the end turn into your world.

Gets Things Done

This is most likely the one advantage of being engaged that we as a whole vibe in our day by day life. In the event that you remain focused, there is a superior shot of you having the capacity to get done with something you began or finish something that you should do. Any individual who isn't engaged has a tendency to defer the errand to some following day or other time and therefore, the task stays fixed. Being engaged is a request of each calling and each field of life. In each and every circle of life, you should be engaged to complete the main priority.

Creates Fulfillment

Remaining concentrated additionally influences you to feel content with yourself and every other person around you. On the off chance that you are not focused around a certain something and your psyche is continually meandering near, you will have more weight and weight at the forefront of your thoughts and body. This denies you of any peace that you could seek after.

When you're engaged, you can simply keep one thing before your eyes and work on it perseveringly. Your cerebrum and body will be in a state of harmony with what you have to achieve at that given time.

Builds Momentum

Focus builds viability which thusly gives you a chance to advance speedier with your assignments. The speedier you get your booked assignments off the beaten path, the more prominent your efficiency.

Focus based force likewise encourages you remain on track and counteracts crashing. Then again, altering course flattens force and irritates focus too. This point can likewise tie in with multitasking where you might endeavor to complete excessively at one time, and each assignment endures. So to remain in force, begin a vocation on time, complete everything the path through and after that proceed onward to the following errand.

Reduces Pressure

Remaining concentrated likewise decreases worry as all your focus will be on the job needing to be done. An absence of focus, then again, prompts getting to be overpowered with an excessive amount to do and too brief period.

Being overpowered additionally hinders your judgment on where to begin and that can be unpleasant as well. With focus, lucidity winds up enhanced, enables you to escape overpower which, thus decreases pressure and prompts enhanced results.

With lucidity in place, you can see the improvement you are making and will work with focus to accomplish your coveted outcomes.

Expands Engagement

Focus provides guidance and reason to an assignment. In this sense it connects with the intrigue and exertion of the person. With an obvious focus in locate, you won't be reluctant to invest extra exertion, since the vast majority are not apprehensive of diligent work but rather the likelihood of disappointment.

At the point when objectives are not explained, it turns out to be hard and even difficult to focus around how to accomplish them. So focus arranged course will provoke intrigue and engagement in all situations.

What the vast majority have in a similar manner as effective individuals is desire, yet where certain miss the mark and others exceed expectations is in the region of self-restraint.

As per Dennis Prager, "Bliss is reliant on self-restraint." The greatest obstacle in accomplishing our objectives is the manner by which effortlessly we let ourselves be occupied by things that don't consider advance towards our accomplishments.

In any case, rehearsing self-restraint isn't simple and requests genuine duty. So as to create self-control, you should take after specific advances that will enable you to achieve your objectives. Here are the best propensities for effective individuals that assistance that keep up self-control which eventually encourages them accomplish their objectives:

Exceedingly effective individuals know precisely where they need to be throughout everyday life. They know precisely where you need to go. It is difficult to be fruitful without knowing where you need to be.

Keeping in mind the end goal to be effective, make a dream board. Clergyman pictures and statements that spur you to accomplish what you need to and take a gander at it before you begin your day. This will enable you to adjust your assignments to your objectives. With a specific end goal to picture, you should have a cognizant deliberateness which causes you in clearing up your head space.

Something else about self-taught individuals is that they complete their imperative tasks previously they permit themselves any liberalities.

It is essential to organize everything with the goal that you confront less diversion amid your day. Completing imperative assignments initially mitigates the weight of a fixed errand and furthermore gives you a lot of time to be beneficial for whatever is left of the day.

For example, if taking a shot at your next task will enable you to be effective in future then it is essential you chip away at it before you let yourself invest energy with companions, on your telephone and so on. As the expression goes, "Being sluggish is the best reward for completing tasks now."

Saying No to Distractions

The most grounded propensity for exceedingly effective individuals is their boldness to state no to diversions. Effective individuals are similarly as inclined to get occupied by online networking and home bases as you yet they square up and say no so as to progress in the direction of their objectives. This does not mean you can never enjoy with online networking nearness or go out with companions yet organizing your work is imperative.

Numerous individuals do not have the mettle to state no to a hang out when they know they ought to work. When you have figured out how to state you will see that you are moving towards your objectives. It is so natural to get diverted by individuals who are chilling however "Don't get occupied by individuals who are not on track."

Handle One Assignment at Any Given Moment

Exceedingly effective individuals are reasonable with their daily agendas. In the event that you have spent a ton of your days hesitating then it is difficult to all of a sudden complete the process of everything in a day. Begin by attempting to focus around one task at any given moment as opposed to overpowering yourself with the possibility of everything that isn't done.

"On the off chance that the end goal feels too far away, don't take a gander at it." Keep yourself concentrated on what you have close by and ensure that you put forth a valiant effort while you are busy.

When you have a greater objective as a top priority it is critical that you partition it in littler lumps. You have to know every one of the means that you should take keeping in mind the end goal to accomplish what you need. Rather than moping around, get reasonable. Partition your objective into what should be done every day, every week, every month or in a half year.

"An objective without design is only a desire." You can't anticipate that all that you need will mystically show up before you. It takes diligent work and each fruitful individual in history put that diligent work in to transform their fantasies into reality.

Rewards and Breaks

You can't remain focused unless you give yourself adequate breaks amid the day. Each business, school or work environment has breaks after a specific period on the grounds that the body can't work persistently for so long without resting. So in the event that you need to keep diversions under control, it is fundamental to take breaks amid the day or working period.

It is vital that you recognize your diligent work on the grounds that your brain will probably remain concentrated on objectives when you give it breaks. Else you will physically and rationally feel overpowered and consume yourself out.

After every day of doing what you expected to, remunerate yourself with a hour of online networking, supper with companions or simply remaining in and chilling without anyone else. This will likewise invigorate you and persuade you to work the following day.

Ensure that you take one day every week where you don't do anything. This is vital keeping in mind the end goal to offer you a reprieve before you begin working once more.

Learn from Mistakes

Something else that exceedingly effective individuals do is gain from their oversights as opposed to stopping. So consider the possibility that you committed an error. It just adds to your experience and shows you about how to move things better.

Each time you commit an error, advise yourself that it is a gift. The more oversights you influence the more you to take yourself on the correct way. Each objective is a gathering of lessons that you gained from your slip-ups en route.

Rise Above Your Feelings

When we realize what we have to do our sentiments can be infectious and beguiling. We can influence ourselves to trust that we can enjoy a reprieve following one day of buckling down or two days of buckling down. Consistency is the way to accomplishment.

Try not to contend with the arrangement you have made for yourself. It is just ongoing to deny diligent work since we wind up acquainted with apathy. On the off chance that you need to accomplish something don't be aloof to sentiments that prompt decimation of your arrangement.

You will have a lot of time for sluggishness and exhaustion when you are finished with your assignments.

Love What You Do

It is critical that you take a gander at diligent work as a positive attribute as opposed to something that strains you. When we constrain ourselves to buckle down it is normal to abhor it since we can't dawdle any longer. Effective individuals cherish their work and consequently it is less demanding for them to invest the exertion that is expected to accomplish their objectives.

At whatever point you feel bothered due to all that you have to complete, remind yourself why you are doing it in any case. This will enable you to build up an inspirational outlook towards your work.

Self-restrained individuals don't consume themselves out. Rather, they commit their push to tasks that need vitality. At times individuals wrongly build up all their vitality for an errand that does not require as much vitality and later they feel worn out or exhausted on the grounds that they utilized everything up.

To accomplish your objectives, realize what requests your dynamic inspiration and what you can manage without utilizing exertion. This is a troublesome task for the individuals who are beginning from zero hence begin by taking up one errand and idealizing it until the point that it moves toward becoming propensity.

At that point include another and gradually develop to it. "Unwind yet don't get excessively agreeable." Your brain will trick you into trusting that you have completed a ton when you accomplish one objective yet it isn't generally valid.

Basically, you can continue perusing tips on self-restraint yet the genuine exertion is to apply them, all things considered. Rather than glancing around for more tips, begin honing them now.

As maybe one of his most well known expressions, Steve Jobs stated, "If today were the latest day of your life, would you need to do what you are going to do?"

Continuously look forward in future. On the off chance that you long for progress then the time has come to push away every one of your diversions and begin chipping away at your objectives.

Regardless of whether you are an understudy, a parent or a laborer, you know about the significance of focus for everything that you do in your life. Regardless of whether there is a fleeting arrangement to take after, or a long haul objective neither can be expert without focus.

There are a couple of systems that you can use to assemble unbreakable core interest. When you prevail with regards to making these procedures a piece of your life, you will be considerably more in contact with yourself and you will encounter a self of achievement that nothing else can give you.

Prepare Your Mind

This is the most fundamental piece of the concentration building process. Your mind controls everything that goes ahead in your body. Regardless of whether it is something you think or something you see or it is something that you feel, everything is controlled by your cerebrum. This is the reason you need broad control over your cerebrum and you have to prepare it to remain focused.

Influence a propensity for rehashing the job needing to be done, to yourself to over and over. Set yourself up rationally for what you are going to do. Before you do anything, sit in a calm place and let it sink into your mind that you will spend the following couple of hours on a particular assignment. This is a mind reinforcing exercise that you have to do to keep focused. In the event that you prepare your mind, it won't be derailed by any diversions after that.

Plan Everything Out

Before you begin anything, you have to design everything out. This does apply to ordinary tasks as well as applies to long haul errands. For instance, organizations that have a tendency to have marketable strategy for a year or a semester have a superior shot of expanding deals and making a stamp. When you design something, you lay every one of the tasks out before you.

This makes it less demanding for you to figure out which things require your most extreme consideration. Utilizing this arrangement, you can likewise plan the time for the fruition of your assignment and you can partition each errand of yours into time interims.

When you realize that you need to complete a specific task in a given time span, you will have the capacity to keep up your concentration better.

Rest for Some Time

The human body isn't made for working always, which is the reason the idea of rest is available in the body. Regardless of how much function should be done, you have to rest for some time. Take a thirty minutes break after each 4 or 5 hours that you work. This would spruce up your cerebrum and it will likewise give you an opportunity to unwind. Amid this time, you can clear your cerebrum and essentially offer uninterrupted alone time.

By resting or taking breaks, you can rapidly develop focus. This system has turned out to be effective even by logical techniques.

Work environments have a meal break and different breaks amid the day with the goal that representatives can remain profitable for the entire day. This is especially vital in the event that you are completing a broad movement. It winds up harder to concentrate so you have to give your cerebrum and body a break. In these couple of minutes or 30 minutes, do what calms your body. Tune in to quieting music or just go for a stroll in some quiet neighborhood.

Work with Music

This procedure may not work with everybody but rather it has appeared to be fruitful as a rule. Tuning in to music is something the vast majority appreciate. You could attempt by playing your most loved music out of sight while you work. It is better if the tune isn't too boisterous in light of the fact that that can cause diversion.

The music must not be too uproarious to divert you from the work that you are doing. Nonetheless, individuals who are inclined to moving around with their most loved music on may not profit by this technique to such an extent.

Practice Mindfulness

Utilizing care to assemble focus is most likely a standout amongst other procedures. The key advance included is to sit in a calm place and take a profound take in. From that point onward, you are required to hold your breath for a couple of moments and afterward breathe out. It is amid this interruption that you have to take your brain back to the thing that it should be on.

Your mind tends to float away from time to time in light of the fact that the life expectancy of human fixation is only 8 seconds. It is because of this reason you have to make this activity a propensity so you can profit by it. It likewise fills in as a reliever of stress and can free the body of any negative vitality. When you harbor positive vitality in the body and you move your cerebrum's capacity to one assignment, your concentration will naturally make strides.

Since we are on the whole animals of propensity, coordinating the correct propensities into your workday will help colossally. When something turns into a propensity, it additionally turns out to be simple. On the off chance that focusing turns into a propensity, it will come to you normally and will give you a chance to have numerous advantages once a day.

Limit Telephone Use

A noteworthy diversion for some, individuals is wireless use and versatile innovation. It can undoubtedly divert you from the errand that you should do.

Most understudies can identify with circumstances where they have assignments or pending tasks yet rather, they are occupied on their PDAs.

So while you are working, ensure that you put your telephone away to abstain from being occupied by approaching calls or messages. On the off chance that you deal with your telephone, introduce an application which gives you a chance to square notices from online networking destinations.

In cases where you don't have a particular work to do on the telephone, there can even now be a slant to utilize it for online networking. This is something else that can occupy you from your errand and at last your objectives.

Set a period for utilizing your telephone. At some point at night or after supper is a decent timeslot for this kind of action. The vast majority are finished with their day's worth of effort by supper time and may utilize their telephone as much as they need.

Give Steady Updates

Another approach to dispose of diversions is to always remind yourself about your objectives and points that you want to achieve. When you do that, you will be slanted towards doing what you really need to do as opposed to squandering your opportunity on pointless things.

Any businessman or individual planning to make a stamp continually helps himself to remember the objective he is wanting to accomplish. A day by day update before anything else is a decent place to begin.

Plan Your Day

Another approach to keep diversions away is to design your day previously. When you go to bed, make a propensity to make a little arrangement for the following day in your brain. Keep the pointless things out of it and ensure that you deal with the things as indicated by the measure of time you have staring you in the face and the errand that should be done first.

When you do as such, your cerebrum will gradually be prepared to just focus on the assignments that you have made arrangements for that day. It is additionally helpful to have an organizer or a journal that you can keep with you. Individuals who have a journal are more sorted out and they have a tendency to accomplish more work on time.

When you make this a propensity, you will have the capacity to adhere to your timetable. It is the hardest to not veer off from the arrangement but rather with training, it can turn out to be second nature. This propensity can prompt achievement and your mind will consequently counterbalance any task it finds pointless that is, any errand not specified in the arrangement.

Having positive vitality is vital as it empowers the body for working in the most ideal way that is available.

Chapter 7 - Why Should You Focus on One Thing At A Time?

Multitasking is essentially attempting to part focus and gap your thoughtfulness regarding completing different tasks at once. While numerous trust that this training really accomplishes more, that may not generally be the situation. Rather, while attempting to build the amount of employments being performed, you may well bargain the nature of each one of them.

The outcome is harming your own particular efficiency while moving concentration from one assignment to the next without being completely mindful to any single one. Rather, here is a glance at why you should just spotlight on one thing at any given moment.

It Completes Things

The best part about completing one thing at once is that it completes things. When you concentrate all your consideration and your vitality to one thing, you guarantee that the specific assignment will complete and it will be done on time. For you to achieve any task, you need intemperate core interest. The thing about concentration is that it gets redirected effortlessly if there are more things at the forefront of your thoughts.

When you are completing one thing at once, your attention is just on that one task and it completes in a convenient way. Despite what might be expected, on the off chance that you attempt to complete three things in the meantime, at that point your concentration will be separated amongst them and you won't have the capacity to do any single one of them.

It Leaves Less Room for Mistakes

Everybody who accomplishes in excess of one thing at a solitary time realizes that there is a considerably more noteworthy possibility of mistake when you are accomplishing more things at one time. Then again, when you give your full focus on one thing no one but you can do it with considerably more precision. Truth be told, multitasking is really exchanging amongst errands and when it comes down to fixation and efficiency, the cerebrum just has a restricted sum.

A typical case is individuals utilizing their PDAs while driving. Since you are not concentrating on one thing just, there is a colossal edge for mistake. Indeed, even in less affecting issues, for example, messaging, this marvel can be seen. On the off chance that you message four or five individuals in the meantime, there is a probability that you will wind up sending the wrong thing to the wrong individual. It is because of this reason you have to maintain your attention on one thing as it were.

Achievement of errands ought not be your exclusive objective. Your objective ought to be to do the assignment in the most ideal route conceivable with least mistake. To make this conceivable, it is basic to remain concentrated on one thing at a solitary time and not have various activities in the meantime.

Higher Achievement Rate

In the event that you focus around one thing at any given moment, you wind up having a superior shot of prevailing at something. This isn't just relevant on account of organizations or business visionaries yet in addition in any regular circumstance. Individuals who endeavor to do just a single thing at any given moment will probably be mindful too than the individuals who attempt to do everything in the meantime.

Similarly, the likelihood of being effective is higher on the off chance that you focus around one thing at any given moment. Organizations tend to focus around one thing for the present, for example, making their promoting more effective or expanding worker efficiency as opposed to attempting to do these things without a moment's delay. It isn't conceivable to juggle such a large number of things without a moment's delay so the better approach is to approach slowly and carefully.

It Doesn't Exhaust Energy

On the off chance that you have a propensity for doing numerous things at one time, you will dependably be drained and will experience the ill effects of an absence of vitality. This is the reason it is smarter to focus around one thing as opposed to attempting to go for three or four things.

The human mind might resemble a machine with regards to its usefulness yet it has the human character of tiredness.

It gets worn out after extended periods of movement or subsequent to doing numerous things in the meantime. When you endeavor to complete a considerable measure of things in the meantime, you are putting a ton of strain on the cerebrum. Subsequently, the vitality stores of the body are abused which prompts a reduction in the vitality levels of the body.

You may feel that you can do numerous things in the meantime yet in all actuality the inner working of your body isn't completely undetectable to you. Along these lines, you can't generally know how an action is hurting within your body.

In the event that you focus around one thing at any given moment, you can guide your mind to do a similar thing for an exact time frame. At the point when your cerebrum just needs to achieve one task at any given moment, it can work all the more viably. Nonetheless, on the off chance that you are endeavoring to cook, clean and compose an article in the meantime, the cerebrum and body will experience serious difficulties attempting to stay aware of the levels of your movement.

On the off chance that your work includes physical work, it can likewise tire out your body and when the body isn't dynamic, its absolutely impossible you can focus around an errand to make it more effective. At the point when your glucose levels run out, your body work additionally diminishes.

It Keeps Diversions Away

Another advantage of completing one thing at once is that it keeps diversions under control. When you attempt to accomplish in excess of one assignment at any given moment, you will discover your cerebrum straying to the next errand that should be finished. Utilizing the illustration specified above, in the event that you are attempting to cook yet your mind is continually focused around the substance you requirement for your article, it isn't far-fetched that you will be effective in any of your assignments.

You might have the capacity to cook and complete your article however the exposition won't be the best you have ever composed and the cooking won't be agreeable. When you concentrate all your consideration and focus onto a certain something, you can without much of a stretch achieve your task as your cerebrum is just reasoning of the present main job.

It Gives You A Chance to Appreciate Your Work

How about we let it out. On the off chance that you are attempting to juggle an excessive number of things in the meantime, you won't have the capacity to appreciate any of it. Simply envision composition messages while eating. It is highly unlikely you will appreciate your supper because of the diversion and it is likewise plausible that you will wind up committing errors in your messages.

Thus, at work or amid considering, in the event that you don't focus around one thing at any given moment, you won't have the capacity to appreciate it. A great many people despise their work since they are attempting to deal with a mess of errands without a moment's delay. When you begin completing one thing at once, you will discover the procedure more agreeable and less demanding to achieve.

Indisputably, multitasking can end up being entirely useless as lower quality work is delivered, more oversights are set aside a few minutes and exertion get squandered.

The hardest thing for a great many people is to live right now. It has turned out to be hard to remain concentrated on one assignment with such huge numbers of diversions around us. In any case, this kind of way of life additionally influences our proficiency at the work environment as our mind meanders and we battle to complete our tasks on time.

Be that as it may, while the web has furnished us with different diversions in type of online networking it has likewise produced instruments which can be useful in arranging time and completing assignments on time. Here is a rundown of a few applications that will enable you to recapture your laser focus and control your chance as opposed to giving web diversions a chance to control it:

1.   StayFocused

StayFocused is an expansion that takes a shot at Chrome. There are numerous advertisement blockers or site blockers that can be added to Chrome. Be that as it may, this one is intended to enable you to complete work as opposed to investing hours on Twitter or Facebook. You can likewise set break times which implies you can set time where you will be permitted to enter sites however when your break time is over you won't be permitted to enter them once more.

The "Atomic Option" is for the individuals who totally can't avoid their diversions. This won't let you enter any of the sites that shield you from working and it can't be deactivated until after the given day and age.

2.   Freedom

This is an application for web, pc, iOS and Mac that can be introduced to shut out sites that divert you so you can focus on what should be finished. Making plan for the day is fun yet completing everything on your daily agenda is a test when you have a propensity for investing hours looking through your most loved web-based social networking.

Flexibility gives you a chance to oversee plans so you can obstruct certain sites for a specific day and age. For example, in the event that you invest hours looking through Facebook, you can include it Freedom application to square it from 9:00 AM to 2:00 PM while you complete your work. Flexibility won't let you enter the place that is known for diversion inside the booked time.

It additionally has a "Bolted Mode" which can be diverted on to keep from breaking the given timetable and surrendering to your desire for online networking. When you have a propensity for stalling, it is difficult to abstain from backpedaling to that way of life however with bolted mode you can without much of a stretch dodge it.

3.	FocusWriter

This application is for those whose work requires a considerable measure of composing. In any case, numerous authors battle with concentrating on their written work while chipping away at their workstations. On the off chance that you likewise battle with remaining concentrated on your work then this is an incredible site which flies up a plain dim foundation to compose on and everything else is blocked away including clock and date until the point when your planned time is finished.

FocusWriter likewise incorporates highlights like word tally and spell-check which are pivotal to composing employments and assignments. It likewise has certain different highlights like defining a written work objective which will bring delight once you have accomplished your objective. Other than that the typewriting sounds with each key make it intriguing to work with FocusWriter.

4.   Concentrate

This application is intended to oversee distinctive kinds of assignments. Infrequently individuals can begin their day extremely propelled to complete everything except for after one errand they have a tendency to get occupied before they can begin the following assignment. Focus will shut out the email customer and program to keep you far from Buzzfeed, YouTube, Twitter and so on while you are composing. Dispatch applications highlight enables you to get to just the applications that are required for errands close by.

The "Talk a Message" highlight enables you to record a message that will play on set time and inspire you to focus on your work. This Mac application is intended to enable you to adhere to your timetable for the day until the point that you have completed the process of everything.

5.   Be Focused

Be Focused application utilizes Pomodro system since it has been demonstrated that individuals tend to focus around their tasks better in the event that they take softens up between. Numerous individuals battle to take a break from dread of losing consideration yet they wind up losing focus with time. Be Focused will give you short breaks following 25 minutes of working and longer interims previously you change starting with one assignment then onto the next.

You can make a rundown of errands and keep tabs on your development as you move along. This iOS application is flawless on the off chance that you would prefer not to lose excitement as you advance. You will inspire time to restore your head space and be prepared to take up the following assignment proficiently.

6.   Forest

On the off chance that you have an inclination that your telephone is anchored to your hands and shield you from working at that point Forest application will enable you to abandon it be while you complete your work. This is an intriguing application that enables you to grow a woodland. At whatever point you enact it, you plant a tree and the tree will kick the bucket on the off chance that you hinder or deactivate.

Woodland application has joined forces with Trees for the Future and each tree you make is really being planted on the planet. This implies each tree you plant will win you virtual coins which will be spent on manor of trees.

7.   Hold

Hold is an application that is uncommonly intended for understudies and watches out for their action. On the off chance that you battle with considering or complete your papers since you can't avoid Instagram encourage and Facebook remarks then this application is for you. For at regular intervals that you spend far from your telephone, you acquire a point.

When you have earned fifteen focuses you get a reward fit as a fiddle of wager tickets or espresso from 7-eleven. Numerous understudies who have utilized this application affirmed that their evaluations enhanced by utilizing the Hold application.

8.   Noisli

A few people tend to concentrate better on their application when they are encompassed by a perfect mood. Noisli gives surrounding clamors like shoreline, blaze crackles, fan and so forth so you can redo a blend of your most loved sounds so you can have the ideal environment to work in.

Noisli is in this manner an application for the individuals who need to work in a specific situation which will enable them to remain concentrated on the task. Noisli likewise has another component roused by Pomodro methods which causes you isolate your errands and Chromotherapy enlivened element gives you a chance to pick a specific foundation shading while you work.

9.   Balanced

Adjusted is an application that encourages you assemble your concentration by making an adjust in your life. It is critical that you keep up a solid way of life that comprises of perusing, contemplation, exercise, strolling and so forth. Adjusted tracks your opportunity spent on doing things that you wish you accomplished more.

A few people battle with perusing books while other can't remain concentrated on yoga. Adjusted will keep you spurred to incorporate these tasks in your every day life and remain concentrated on them.

10.   Hocus Focus

Hocus Focus is another application made to enhance your profitability by influencing your program tab to mess free. Its a dependable fact that we tend to concentrate better when we have a cleaner domain. The same is valid about dealing with your PC.

Hocus Pocus will close any site that you are not currently utilizing. For example on the off chance that you have diverting applications like Twitter, Buzzfeed, Facebook and so forth open out of sight then they will stop while you begin working. An exploration demonstrates that it takes 23 minutes for a normal human cerebrum to refocus and a diverting application can make it significantly harder.

Thanks again for buying my book. If you have a minute, please leave a positive review. You can leave your review by clicking on this link:

Leave your review here. Thank you!

I take reviews seriously and always look at them. This way, you are helping me provide you better content that you will LOVE in the future. A review doesn't have to be long, just one or two sentences and a number of stars you find appropriate (hopefully 5 of course).

Also, if I think your review is useful, I will mark it as "helpful." This will help you become more known on Amazon as a decent reviewer, and will ensure that more authors will contact you with free e-books in the future. This is how we can help each other.

DISCLAIMER: This information is provided "as is." The author, publishers and/or marketers of this information disclaim any loss or liability, either directly or indirectly as a consequence of applying the information presented herein, or in regard to the use and application of said information. No guarantee is given, either expressed or implied, in regard to the merchantability, accuracy, or acceptability of the information. The pages within this e-book have been copyrighted.